Adv

"In *Golden Hour*, Ley Matutina explores the love we feel for others and, most importantly, the love we cultivate for ourselves. Her poetry takes readers on a journey that begins as an intimate whisper of self-acceptance, before erupting into a powerful declaration. Through evocative verses, this collection illuminates the complexities of connection, revealing the tender intensity of love that can be both warm and cold. Matutina encourages readers to recycle their pain into strength and embrace the fleeting light of Now. This collection is a celebration of self-love and resilience, reminding us that even in twilight, there is beauty to be found."
— Renzo Del Castillo, Award-Winning Author of *Still*

"Matutina's poetry collection, *Golden Hour*, shows the vulnerability and rawness of fighting demons stemming from emotional attachment. It is an inspiring work of art that encompasses the fear of abandonment and the mystery of potential relationships."
— Valeria Abelli, Author of *Closure*

"*Golden Hour* is a gorgeous journey about the avenues love takes you, allowing you to experience feelings and journeys that fall apart and rise again, like dusk and dawn. I love the relatability of circling thoughts and phases we approach when it comes to the depths or lack of loving."
— Kendall Hope, Author of *Tongue Tied*

"*Golden Hour* is a warm embrace that leaves you feeling loved. It is a poetry collection, complete with illustrations, that will have you learning to let go of old loves and patterns and welcoming in new ones, especially when it comes to self-love and self-acceptance."
— Flor Ana, Author of *The Truth About Love*

Copyright © 2024 by Leydi Arboleda

All rights reserved.

This book (or any portion thereof) may not be reproduced or used in any manner without written permission from the author except in the context of reviews.

Cover Art Copyright © 2024 by Leydi Arboleda x Indie Earth
Illustrations Copyright © 2024 by Leydi Arboleda

Edited by Leydi Arboleda and Flor Ana Mireles

1st Edition | 01
Paperback ISBN: 979-8-9912164-6-3

First Published November 2024

For inquiries and bulk orders, please email:
indieearthpublishinghouse@gmail.com

Printed in the United States of America   1 2 3 4 5 6 7 8 9

Indie Earth Publishing Inc.
| Miami, FL |

www.indieearthbooks.com

GOLDEN HOUR

Ley Matutina

*To my mom,
whom although this book is not about,
I write because she always asked me to.
I write,
and from now on
and especially the one to come,
I will honor her
and thank her in hindsight.*

GOLDEN HOUR

TABLE OF CONTENTS

SUNRISE ... 1

TWILIGHT ... 17

SUNSET ... 31

DUSK ... 45

DARK ... 59

DAWN ... 73

GOLDEN HOUR ... 89

SUNRISE

SUNRISE

The start of something
is always joyful,
beautiful,
happy.
You smile over dumb things,
you're playful,
humorous,
sappy.
- *"honeymoon" phase*

I look up and wonder
what do those eyes hide?
If all the mystery behind you
is due to you feeling
the same way as I do,
and stopping yourself
for the exact same reason.

I wonder if hearing from me
brings the same smile to your face
that it brings to mine,
and if you are aware
that the smooth little comments you make,
make my day.

I wonder too:
are you trying to run away from this,
as much as I am?
- IV/I

Their actions were restrained,
by the awareness of each other
wanting to make the first move.
She, not wanting to start
something she knew
she couldn't finish.
He, tempting and touching
but not taking it further,
feeling satisfied enough
to finally be able to
hold her in his arms.

It felt like a forbidden love,
and they both liked that
- Feb 23rd.

We were drawing a map,
tracing the lines of our bodies,
figuring out the place we wanted
in each other's worlds . . .
The thing about cartography,
is that we become aware
of the near impossibility
of setting boundaries
once the lines drawn
have been crossed.
- April 23rd

SUNRISE

There are such things
that will never stop being beautiful,
like hearing your name from strangers.
But from lovers,
I want much more intimacy
when they call out my name.
like that we'd share
behind closed doors.
Like that we'd share
when he whispers in my ear,
my name rolling out of his tongue.
Whomever he is,
and who he can be.
When he traces my body with his fingers,
and let's me trace his hair with mine…
When love will become
meaningful again
and we both come undone.
- January 20th.

I'll never forget
how you took me by surprise
when you finally asked,
because in all honesty,
I had given up
on any thoughts of you and I.
- III/IV

As he had his forehead
pressed against mine
I felt it all.
The flutter of his eyelashes,
the quick pace
of his heartbeat . . .
But most of all
that sweet,
little tilt of his lips,
that made my heart flutter,
because I knew
the reason for that smile
was me.
- *our little bubble bubu*

The first one
wasn't necessarily movie standard.
It was far less, and much more.
The worry in his actions,
the tenderness of his touch,
the love in his eyes...

We were in synchrony,
but it wasn't until later,
many suns later,
that I understood that the synchrony
was meant to form a symphony,
in which, when you open your eyes,
you see yourself ignite.
- immortalization

Soft lips caressing my neck,
while his fingers roam my body.
His skilled touch
and comforting whispering,
his unsteady breathing
and his intoxicating smell and taste.
He drives me to the top
and lets me set the pace,
while he whispers in my ear:
"Let me put you to sleep."
- *anonymous*

As I laid on his chest
with my eyes closed
I would trace away
my worries on his body.

I would trace my hand
through every edge, curve, indent
and he would momentarily
put my demons
to rest.
- *power of distraction*

SUNRISE

I noticed he is a gate
to another world,
with new scenery that awaits
to be discovered.
With beautifully new,
yet terrifying,
flora and fauna,
that makes me wonder,
whether all the creatures in it
see me as a predator
or a prey . . .

Am I putting myself in danger?
Either way,
I feel I'm in a dray,
and he is dragging me
to this realm with him.

There is no turning back now.
- May 12th.

TWILIGHT

Most often than not,
love is not what it poses.
As we both know,
is not all butterflies and roses.
Loving is a choice,
and in between loving,
there are always limbos.
So, then,
Is it that love is either:
you make it a permanent home,
or you throw it out the window?
- *the in between*

We have become
the people that we used to abhor.
That instead of seeking peace,
looks for conflict,
wrongly assuming that brute words
will appease the root cause of it,
blinding us,
making us look coarse.
When did you start bringing this side of me out?
the one that I used to come to you
to help me bailout,
the one that I thought
I would never have to be with you.
- *mixed*

I feel your love fading
and I tell myself:
Don't do that!
Don't let that missed date
be "whatever,"
don't look away
when he's talking to other girls.
Don't allow him
to raise his voice at you.
All for what? . . .

Don't hold on too hard,
you'll only hurt yourself.
 - *1. you.*

It is always the same thing.
I sculpt my clay
to look more and more
like what you want of me,
forgetting what my original shape looks like...

What am I doing
trying to appease the unpleasable?
When all you do is push me away.
You push me away
by saying things so carelessly,
by acting with this *superiority*
and then playing the victim,
making yourself feel attacked by me?

It's draining, you know?
You act like you know me,
but honestly,
you just see the side of me
that you want to see,
the one that looks the least like yourself.
 - *April 9th. Her.*

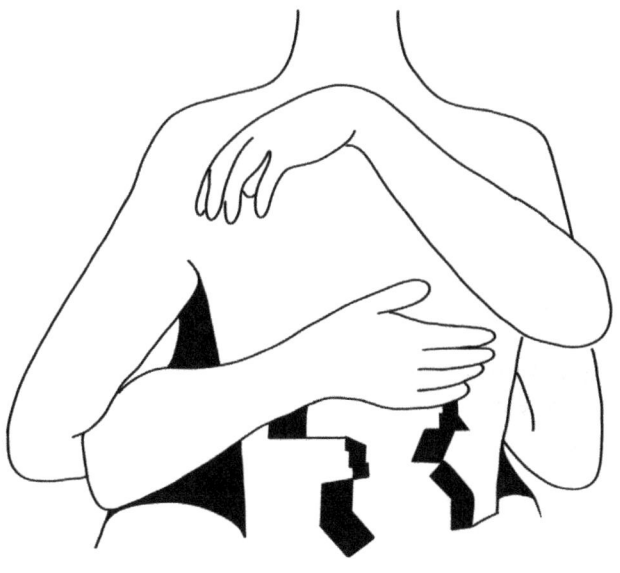

I am not the cure
nor the addiction,
and yet, sometimes I wish
I could be either or.

That all your ailments vanish,
that all your worries perish,
that all your aspirations are accomplished,
when I am with you...
- for you to stay

When I love,
I don't warm,
I burn.

I set myself aflame
to keep others warm.
I extinguish all my air
to keep the flame going,
forgetting I am suffocating me.

But I do so in the hopes
that when my flame dies out
he will be there burning bright for me.
- I, the fool

I am not unbroken.
I've been shattered
by others . . .
a lot of the shattering
was done by you,
but even more, sadly,
by myself.

TWILIGHT 27

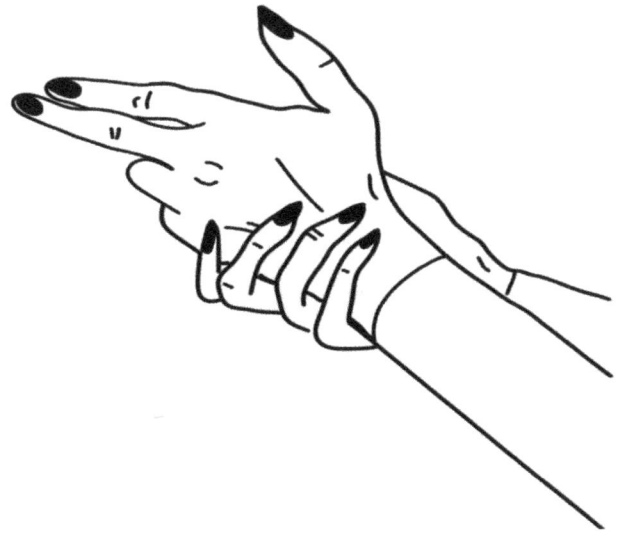

You say you are sensitive
and I am tough.
Don't you realize
that I built my walls
out of the stones thrown at me.
That my colorful self
became acquainted with grey people,
people who did nothing
but exhaust my colors,
while pretending
to be pouring colors back into me,
and now, *I am gray too.*

You may not be a disease
but you are slowly intoxicating me.
Affecting my immune system
with soft words
and soft actions.
Debilitating my walls,
letting you convince me
that things will be different next time,
this time...

But there are aspects of you
that flare up my defense system,
and I have started to become
allergic to your lies,
and immune to your "wisdom."
- April 5th

Even being aware
of how toxic you were to me
my feet felt glued to the ground.

Unwilling to listen to my mind,
that needed space,
unwilling to listen to my heart,
that needed comfort,
unwilling to listen to my body,
that couldn't stand another debate.
- time to go . . .

SUNSET

I had a person.
Someone who had seen
the nakedness of my soul.
Felt the scars from past hurt
in my body,
touch the clothing
of my life stories,
in my skin,
and loved me *whole*.

But at some point,
when he held me,
I felt a void.
An embrace so cold,
and detached
that, although I was warm,
my warmth was not enough
to overcome the chills
that crept up my body
from his embrace.

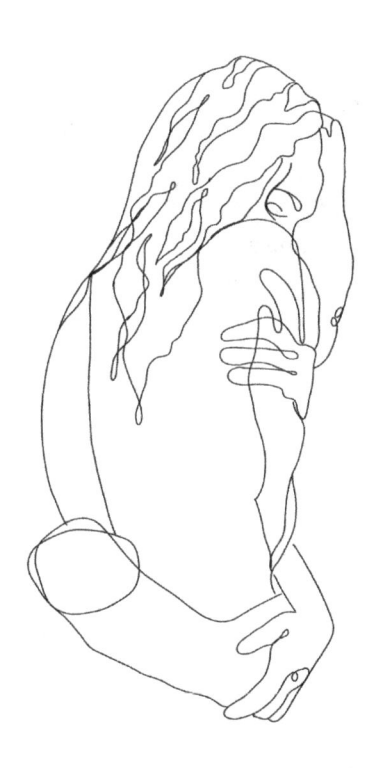

There comes a time
when doing pros and cons
feels like an unbearable weight.
As if deciding
was to seal one's fate,
because no matter how much you tried,
you knew the list was immutable,
unyielding.

For in the twilight of choices,
there was no golden gleam.

No golden hour
to fulfill the dream.
Just the quiet acceptance,
devoid of strife,
as the sun set
on our love's life.

Your love put me under a spell,
blinding me
into a false dichotomy
of believing you were neither
a sanctuary
nor absolute danger.

You had me fooled
thinking
you were somewhere in between.
Somewhere I could rest
my mind, my body, my being,
but as I started to rest,
your love started to wean,
and then you left...

Yet, the consequences of your selfish acts remained.
Tainting me,
leaving me drained,
taunting me,
leaving me unwillingly unconstrained.
- *bitter heart*

I am not going to lie,
I couldn't even call you an ally,
and no matter
whether you had an "alibi,"
I am not gonna let you
 make me the bad guy.

Your departure
was as shocking
as your arrival,
but at least your leaving,
finally felt final.

There was no closure
that could be gained
from the reality
of knowing that you knew
who you were parting with,
and it wasn't me.
- *MMXVII*

Enjoy your privileged life
full of empty words
and fake emotions.
Hope you know
you got a demotion.

Very soon
you'll miss my *rawness*,
and she'll hear you
call out my name.
- *sour patch*

You left me wondering:
how can someone
I have shared
so much intimacy with,
be now so careless?

How did we go
from potential soulmates,
to complete & mere strangers?

That was my biggest disconnect.

When I was little,
I used to dream
that when I got older
I would devour the world.

As I got older,
I felt the world
devouring me;
ripping me into pieces
one at a time...

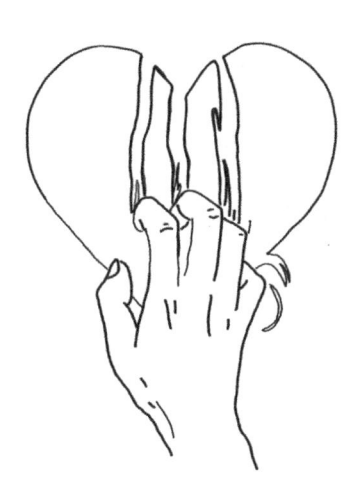

I am not balanced.
I feel in extremes,
and because of it
I searched for my complete opposite:
Composed,
passionate, yet ambitious & focused.
Too much of both,
but always passionate...

I thought he was everything I wasn't
but wanted to be.
And he wanted to teach me...

But what's there to learn
from pretense?
Eventually I realized
anything he said was just common sense.

There was no want
to grow together,
only the distorted optics of "love"
that could be seen if you were clever.
- *I wasn't*

You did not make me,
but you allowed me
to feel less whole.
You were fine with it,
because I continued to pour
until I started
giving you less than before.

Suddenly,
you were no longer fine with it,
because you started feeling
less whole yourself.
So, then you left,
but you do not stay gone . . .

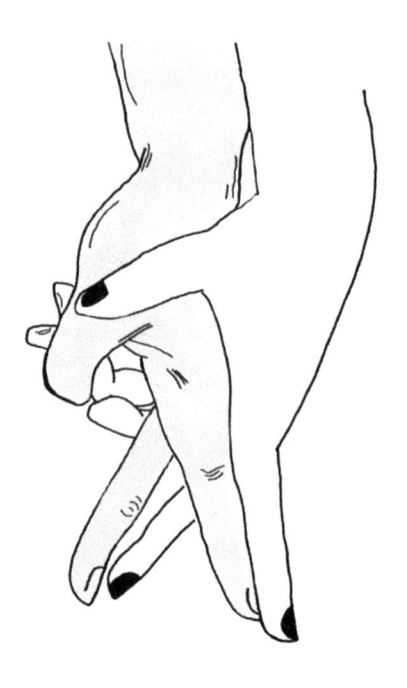

Soft spoken voice
at sporadic hours
that made my heart go erratic
and my mind go numb.

Even at a distance,
that was the hold you had on me.

Why do I still feel
the need to check on you?
It bothers me that seeing
whether you're busy or not,
still makes my heart somersault.

I thought I was past you,
but you have kept up,
and your memory has crept up
like a shadow
materializing,
like a distant dream
revitalizing,
but I am not one to like
surmising. . .
VI/VI

DUSK

I was stuck
between the space of your lips,
not knowing
whether their closing
would hurt me
or make me feel loved by you again.

You held the power to do this to me.

To create a forever unoccupied space
for you to come and go as you pleased,
knowing that I would leave
the door to my heart
 ajar
for you and your cigar.

In that weak limbo
of having you
but not really,
my body wanted you,
but my mind knew
you were not being true.

You were playing the hero,
but I wasn't buying
your tale anymore
because I knew
I was only getting
a ghost of you.

Trying for you to love me
was like digging
for an empty treasure.
No matter how hard I tried
to be close
to that whom you once loved me by,
I couldn't undo what was done,
and you couldn't' love me
like you thought you could.
- May 20th

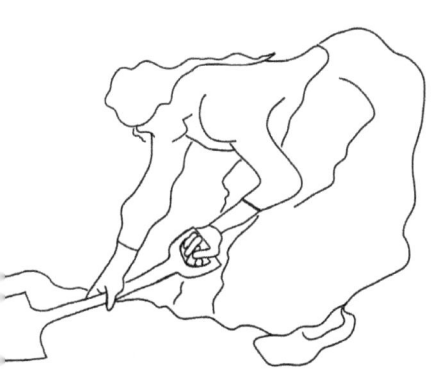

You put me away.

Boxed me,
without a fragile caution sign,
and placed me on the doormat
to be picked up,
and be led astray.

You kicked me out
of my own heart,
as if you were the landlord,
and I,
a mere tenant. . .
an ordinary passerby.
- May 23rd, *cold* heart

Your coming back,
was like a wave.
it's build-up,
magnificent,
it's pace,
controlled and steady...
but eventually,
inevitably chaotic.

You momentarily disturbed
my carefully constructed ecosystem,
which I built up
after you.

But this time your fall out
was nothing but
exceedingly disappointing.
Like the feeling of
skin peeling
after a bad tan...
- April 13th

From time to time,
I miss the warmth of your body
pressed against mine,
sheltering me from the darkness...

I miss being able
to have a brain to pick on,
arms to run to,
hands to hold.

But lonely hearts
and longing bodies,
have no control,
and I don't aim
to find out
whether it was you who won.
- I/XXII

You cannot be caught up
on someone's potential,
because even if you see
all of their exponentials,
they themselves
have yet to discover
they even have these credentials.

You don't know
how long it will take,
nor what obstacles
they'll have to shake,
to make sure
that these "qualities" awake.

So, understand now,
and save yourself the trouble
that you cannot help someone grow,
when they do not want to.

You have loved before them.
And, guess what sweetie?
You will love again.

Let them go.

When it comes to loving others,
I fear love . . .
because I've been in love
and I know how hard it is to leave.

Its more than just the grieve,
but you are also not naïve,
because at that point,
all that's left
are your make-believes.

All you're leaving behind
are the memories,
and the feelings
of either toxicity or sourness
the ending may bring about.

But then,
there also all the beautiful memories made,
fleeting memories that may fade,
but, moments I want forever treasured.

That's what I want
to remember love by,
for all its things,
dear and precious.

Now what I truly seek
is freedom.

Freedom to want nothing,
expect nothing,
depend on nothing.

Not that I won't own anything,
but that nothing
will own me.
- *a selfless love*

My love comes in waves or not at all.
Some, I love vividly and passionately.
Full of details,
with an insatiable wanting
to satisfy their every need,
but hurting my own sometimes . . .

Others,
I love vicariously and from a distance.
thinking that the sporadic acts of love
I do for them,
is enough to remind them
that I love them,
that I care.

This extreme loving is my essence,
my heart's composition:
Beautiful and catastrophic.

Like water,
that just as easily it gives life
it can take it away.

- *I am made of love, love cannot abandon me.*
March 1st.

DARK

As the darkness engulfed me
I was no longer scared,
since I had seen
how equally destructive
the light could be.

I was no longer scared
because I had finally found
a light of my own,
ever present within,
waiting for me to realize
I am not alone.

 I am all that I need.
- *farola*

Dancing sets me on fire.
It fills my soul with desire
to listen to my body
and let it do its thing.

I dance for myself,
but its also something
I get to do with others,
particularly special
to enjoy with lovers.
Bodies touching,
eyes engaging,
souls connecting
to the sync of the heartbeats,
of the music,
of our souls.
- May 3rd

I can be easy going
but I have never been
a "go with the flow"
kind of girl,
and I'm not really sure
if that's been my saving
or my undoing.
- May 15th

Scenarios will occur
where people will be cold,
and places will be too . . .

Don't ever let that coldness
slip into your soul,
and chill your being.
Don't let anything
or anyone
make you into something you are not.
- May 22nd

Set it off,
like I know you can,
like I know you want to,
like you know I want to too.

Be the match
that lights it up,
and sets it all ablaze.

There's a need for change.
- April 22nd

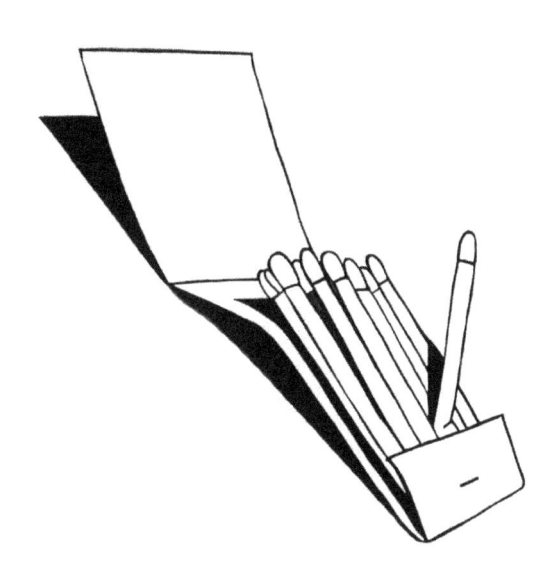

We story-tell through life
in every new and old encounter.
We recall what we've lived,
and what we've learned from it,
either by using others advice,
or advising others.

We share things
 that we have lived alone,
but have experienced together,
and realize we are never as lonely,
as we think ourselves to be.

It's all a little more comforting
once we know
we experience life together,
but not the same.
Once we know that we are alive
alongside millions of other people,
all trying to find ourselves.
- March 25th

I came across me at a crossroad,
and I feared the leap.

Fearing leaving my old self behind,
but knowing
there was much more to find,
so, I jumped.

I jumped
not knowing what was in front
but knowing
that there's so much more of me
that I can become,
and I am ready to discover.

It was the tipping point
of my somewhat,
very carefully,
balanced scale.

Balanced
in that all of my problems,
emotions,
 and responsibilities,
had piled on one side,
and the other
was full of neglect
and procrastination.

The latter outweighed the first
because fear was strongest,
but it all crumbled
when I began to accept
no one is coming to my rescue,
and I have all the power,
to set what happens next.
- March 29th

You change,
but the world
does not change with you.

Understanding that,
is the hardest stage
of your healing process.

That's the stage
that puts you back on your knees
by the feet of those who broke you.

Don't let it!

Don't crawl back,
to those that hurt you,
walk back to yourself.
- III/XXVII

Balance has always been utopian for me.

The status quo says
you are allowed to feel,
but to not feel too much . . .
You can be smart and beautiful,
but not hot and sexy.
It foments individualism,
but then generalizes you
for showing a trait of the collective.

This unachievable set
of contradictions
is not balance.

We are meant to live
in a mixture
of harmony and chaos.
Because that reflects
who we are in our essence:
the fire and ice in our souls.

DAWN

As time has passed,
we both discern,
life hasn't been easy.

There have been
battle wounds
and some hard lessons to learn,
but, like shards
casted into the sea's motion,
the wounds' edges
have dulled with time.

Remember that everything passes.
Don't allow yourself
to keep getting hurt,
by lingering on the pain,
of wounds,
that are now inert.

There's no more getting cut,
by that sea glass' soft edges
- May 21st

Pain is our history
and fortune teller.
It unveils what we've been,
what we are,
and where we could steer.

It shows us
that we have overcome,
and can overcome again.
But also,
that we could surrender,
and although in that
there's not much splendor,
we're not always meant to shine…

Its okay
for our light to falter,
and even decline.
So go ahead,
and rest up.
Then, stand back up
and fight again.

If not, its crucial to know
that you'll be confined
on the wars fought by others
for your life's own command.
- May 29th

It took a treacherous journey
to get closer to where I want to be.

To realize
I was capable of doing
what I sought from others,
on my own.

To have covered,
glued,
and finally
stitched
my broken parts together.
To know what I embody:
Kintsukuroi.

I am the more beautiful
for having been broken,
and putting myself back together.
- March 5th

I live passing the pages behind me,
and without skimming to those ahead,
because days are to be enjoyed,
the cliched present
of the present.

Enjoy the now,
enjoy those around you,
enjoy the scenery,
the glow...

Don't live reminiscing.
what once was,
because you're not guaranteed
what could be.
- April 24th

I cry sometimes in sight now,
because I no longer
want to cry in seclusion.

I laugh at the irony of life
because I am stronger
and I know now,
that it's the best solution.

So, I cry, laugh, love,
and do so unapologetically
because I can,
and because I want to.
Because feeling
is what makes me human,
and that is why
I cry and laugh so much.
- May 9th

I love now
unlike how I loved yesterday,
unlike how I will love tomorrow...

I exude love,
and put love in everything I do.
And now, more than ever
I know that she is the reason
I love the way I do.

She has always been
my regular clothes wearing hero
with her white coat
as her cape,
and her wisdom
as her superpowers.

She helped me see my light,
value what I'm worth.

So, I honor her,
by protecting my patrimony,
myself,
by keeping all the phonies at bay.

- mami, my heart.

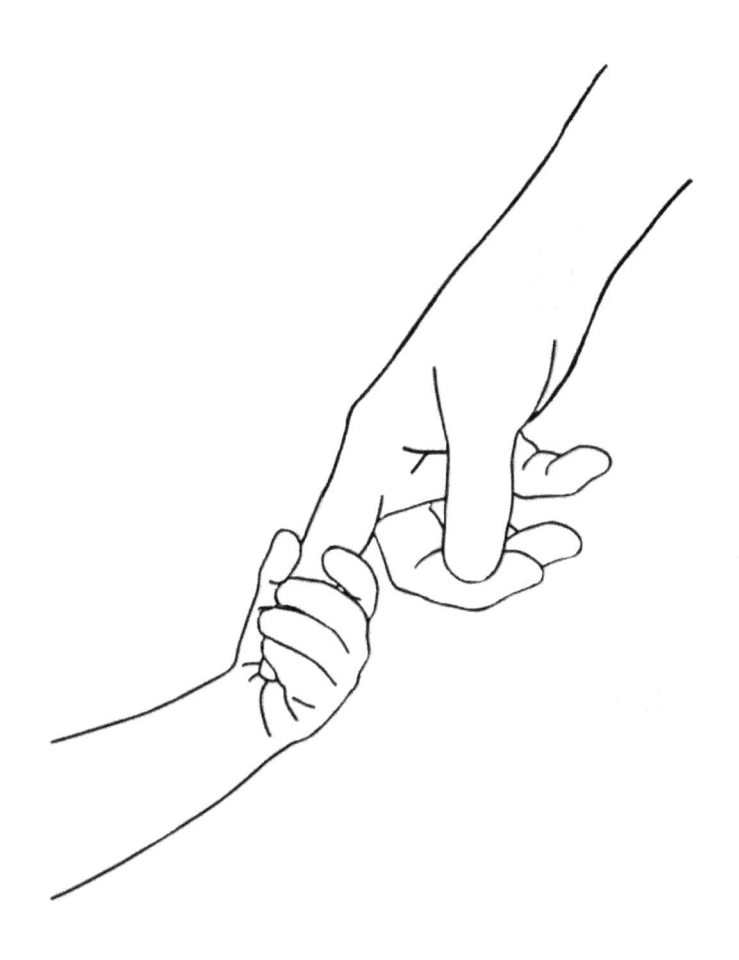

Protect your aura,
because your vibration
is not something to take for granted.
it is something that you have carefully planted,
and continue to cultivate within yourself.

Protect your aura,
and to those that you let around it,
remind them it is their privilege,
and not their right,
to be surrounded by it,
by you.

Be on that
"me, myself, and I"
kind of brag.

I am enrolling
on courses of not caring,
in attempts of mastering
in the art of giving no f***s.
- May 22nd

If you do not see me
because I stopped chasing you,
don't chase me.

If you feel like you want to,
remember it was you
who left.

Now,
I am chasing myself.
and falling in love with me.

Do not disrupt my peace
for your entertainment.

GOLDEN HOUR

I awoke to the realization
that I had been projecting,
trying to have others
fulfill roles they were never meant to…
but, no more.

I take ownership of my actions,
or lack thereof,
of statements of others
that turned into rooted beliefs
of a portrait of myself I never was,
and never will be:
I am not hard to love,
I was just searching for love
in the wrong places.
I am not difficult to understand,
I was just speaking to those
who did not speak my language.
I am not alone
because I have found joy
in my own company,
and in doing so,

I have found my tribe.
I awoke to my power
and realized,
I am capable of change.
I can't control what's coming,
but I trust in my abilities,
to overcome.
 - *confia.*

Recycle your pain.
Use it as fuel
to propel you forward.
Don't let it become an obstacle
revving you aimlessly away.
 - 08/18

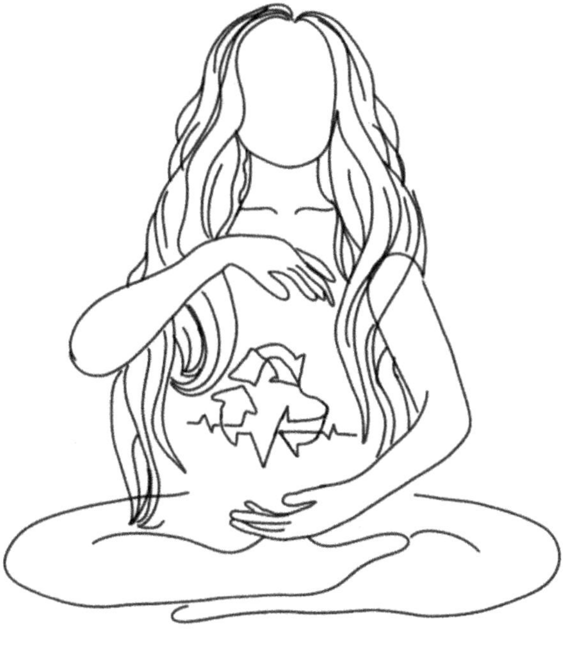

Teach your demons
to fear your name;
to tremble at the sight
of the foundation your laying upright
for yourself
of your confident light

Sometimes in life
we have to pass bumps on the road
to be reminded
of the brevity of our existence.

There are no guaranteed tomorrows...
So stop resisting!

Live for the things
that truly matter,
like those you'd be happy doing
knowing they could be
the last thing you do on this earth.
 - *we are our source of happiness*
so be on a constant
pursuit of yourself.

To live with one's self
is one's greatest challenge
but also
one's greatest joy.

Slowly,
but surely,
you begin to reconnect with yourself.

You understand
that your beliefs of being healed
were truly *you*
coming apart
to come all together.

The breaking
finally let
a crack of light
slip in.

No matter its shape
nor how big or small,
rejoice
in your little beam of sunshine.

GOLDEN HOUR

My growth
has resembled that of my curls
that, like vines
reaching for the sun,
grow with a quiet persistence.

As I watch them grow,
I play around and twist them,
and I question:
> why do we constantly seek out
> what we can find within?

We get tangled in fear
and avoid combing through
because we anticipate coarseness...
But rough textures
lead to higher definition,
and isn't that the goal?
> To wash away our sorrows,
> and condition each strand of our soul
> in this journey
> inward and upward
> until we learn to celebrate
> our natural form.

I have decided
to live more intentionally,
and no longer live
in my what-ifs.

I am thriving in my "mistakes"
because I would rather be
momentarily happy,
spontaneous,
and a little reckless...
than painstakingly bored,
or "safe" & "stable"
yet always helpless.

I owe that to myself,
my loved ones,
& all my prior lives
that have amassed
my spiritual wealth.
 - *I thank you*

Existence is playful.
It invites you to prioritize playtime
or condemn yourself to live
in a constant of everything but play.

So why fight it?
Why categorize things so fast
& so harshly?

Sometimes,
in all that you have deemed too childish
lies the secret to living
happily ever after.

The only move I will make
will be forward.
I will accomplish something small
but significant
every day.

I will rejoice in spontaneity
and in carefully planned things.
I will stop people-pleasing,
second-guessing,
and overanalyzing life.
I will live in the now,
let go of guilt,
and the need to control.

I will try my hardest
to be better every day,
exhausting all means,
but not myself.

I am like a waterfall scenery
        in that, I can bring you serenity
& when present within me,
        you worship my femininity
        because it connects you
        to the divine.

Upon further observation,
        your peripheries notice
        that this connection awakens
        some dangerous grounds in your mind.
Because I am also like a tsunami,
        a reckoning,
        like a wolf
                untamable
        and fiery,
        like the 4th of July,
        and still,
                sweet like honey
                and as homey
                        as a fireplace
                        on a snowy Christmas night.

I am like the ease
        that you feel
        when you're driving into a new street
and suddenly
        all the lights turn green
and you realize
        you'll make it
        right on time.
- I am

In the game of love,
it finally dawned on me,
that I am not a single riddle.
I am the whole set of clues and rewards,
and nowhere in the middle.
I was the seed,
and am now the flower,
this is it for me:
my golden hour.

It was not at the brightest,
but at the first slimmer of light,
after I have learned
I am capable
to co-exist with the dark.
- ley matutina (a.m.)

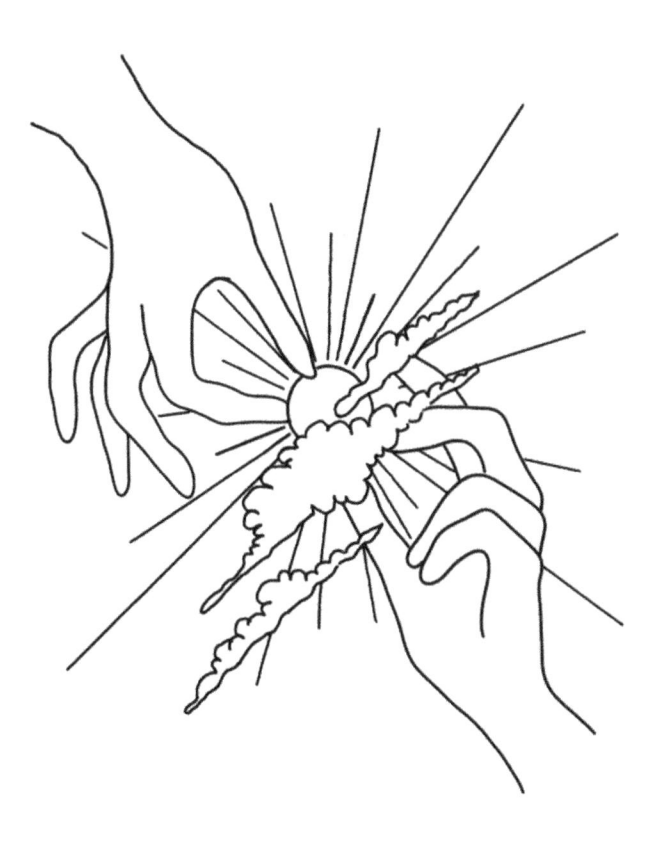

GOLDEN HOUR

Ley Matutina

ABOUT THE AUTHOR

Leydi Arboleda (aka Ley Matutina), is a proud Peruvian who has called Davie and Miami home for the past nine years. After earning her J.D. from Florida International University, she's returning to her true passion: artistic and creative writing. Her debut poetry collection, Golden Hour, beautifully captures the journey of love—from the tender moments we share with others at sunrise to the profound realization that the greatest love we find is within ourselves. Leydi dreams of one day becoming a Poet Laureate and achieving international recognition as a poet.

Connect with Ley Matutina on Instagram:
*@leymatutina_*

ABOUT THE PUBLISHER

Indie Earth Publishing is an independent, author-first co-publishing company based in Miami, FL, dedicated to giving authors and writers the creative freedom they deserve. Indie Earth combines the freedom of self-publishing with the support and backing of traditional publishing for poetry, fiction, and short story collections by providing a plethora of services meant to aid them in the book publishing experience.

With Indie Earth Publishing, you are more than just another author, you are part of the Indie Earth creative family, making a difference one book at a time.

www.indieearthbooks.com

For inquiries, please email:
indieearthpublishinghouse@gmail.com

Instagram: @indieearthbooks

Printed in the USA
CPSIA information can be obtained
at www.ICGtesting.com
LVHW041807301124
797922LV00005B/500